# Electricity Adds

D0732139

by Suzanne Lyons

# Table of Contents

# Introduction

Flash! Lightning streaks across the sky. For an instant, the sky is aglow. What is this phenomenon of nature?

Lightning is electricity. You use electricity daily—when you plug in a toaster, talk on the telephone, or turn on the T.V. Today, electricity powers our world. But it is only recently that people have discovered what electricity really is and how it can be used. In fact, most of the electrical devices we rely on have been invented in the last 75 years.

There are other examples of electricity in nature. Sharks communicate by sending electrical signals through the water. The electric eel makes pulses of electricity to stun its prey and to defend itself. Those pulses are strong enough to kill a horse!

Your body is a busy living factory powered by electricity. For example, when you pick up your backpack, electrical signals travel from your brain along nerve cells in your spinal cord to muscle cells in your arm. When the muscle cells receive the electrical message, they contract and lift the load.

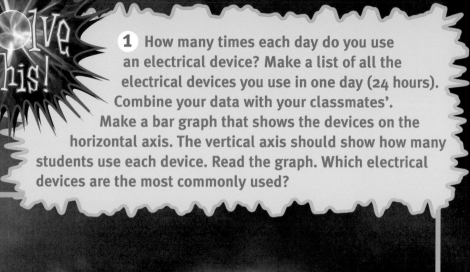

**S lve This!**

**1** How many times each day do you use an electrical device? Make a list of all the electrical devices you use in one day (24 hours). Combine your data with your classmates'.

Make a bar graph that shows the devices on the horizontal axis. The vertical axis should show how many students use each device. Read the graph. Which electrical devices are the most commonly used?

A lightning bolt is an electric discharge.

Electricity makes the lights come on and the Ferris wheel turn.

# What Is Electricity?

**Electrons**, which are tiny particles inside atoms, create electricity. To understand what electricity is, you need to know about atoms and the electrons they contain.

Everything is made up of atoms. There are only about 100 different kinds of atoms in the universe. But atoms combine in different ways to build everything you see, touch, smell, hear, or taste—

from clouds, plastic, and cheddar cheese to your very own skin, brain, and bones.

An atom has a center, or nucleus. Inside the nucleus are particles called neutrons and protons. Different kinds of atoms contain different numbers of protons. They may also contain different numbers of neutrons. Moving around outside the nucleus are the electrons.

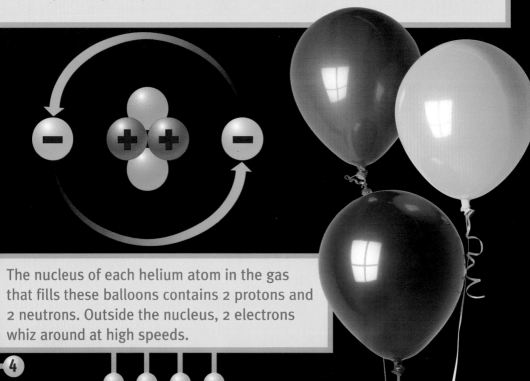

The nucleus of each helium atom in the gas that fills these balloons contains 2 protons and 2 neutrons. Outside the nucleus, 2 electrons whiz around at high speeds.

Atoms are tiny. They are so small that more than a million would be needed to stretch across the width of a human hair! Protons and neutrons are even smaller. Electrons are smaller still.

Some of the particles in atoms have an electric charge. Electrons have a negative (-) electric charge; protons have a positive (+) electric charge. An atom usually contains as many protons as electrons.

Look at the helium atom shown on page 4. Can you see that it has 2 protons and 2 electrons? Each proton has one unit of positive charge and each electron has one unit of negative charge. Thus a helium atom has a total electric charge of $+2 + (-2) = 0$. In other words, the helium atom has zero charge. It is electrically neutral.

**Solve This!**

**2** a. A neutral gold atom contains 79 protons. How many electrons does it contain? b. Atoms sometimes lose electrons. If a neutral atom loses one electron, will it have a positive charge, negative charge, or will it be neutral?

**Opposites Attract**

Objects with an electric charge either attract or repel one another. Particles with the same electric charge repel, or move away from one another. Two positive charges repel each other. Two negative charges also repel each other.

Particles with different electric charges attract. This means that a positive charge and a negative charge attract.

A proton and an electron attract. The diagram below shows how charged objects behave by either attracting or repelling each other.

If you rub a balloon against a wool sweater, the balloon acquires a negative charge. The balloon is then attracted to positive charges in the wall. The balloon sticks to the wall. Try this bit of science "magic" for yourself!

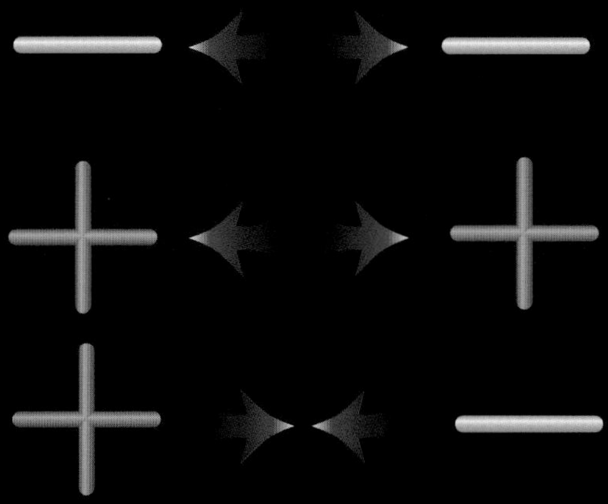

Particles with the same electric charge repel. Particles with different electric charges attract.

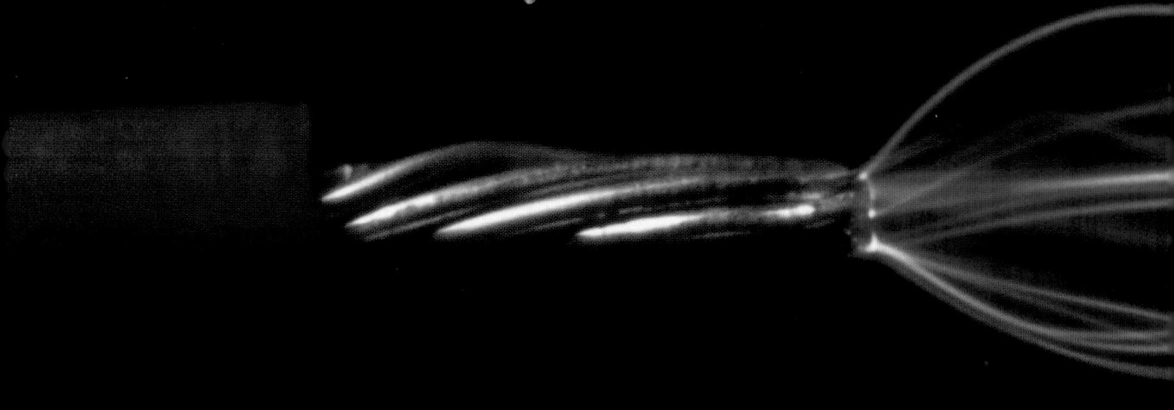

## Static Electricity

Sometimes electric charges build up on an object. The balloon-and-sweater "magic" is an example of this. Negative charges moved from the sweater to the balloon. The charge built up on the balloon and stayed there.

Electric charge that builds up on an object and does not move is called **static electricity**. Perhaps you have seen static electricity build up on clothes in the dryer. Can you think of other examples of static electricity?

Sometimes the transfer of charge is great enough for you to see a spark, hear a crackle, or feel a shock. For example, you can become negatively charged by walking across a carpet if electrons from the carpet build up on you. If you grab a metal doorknob, the electrons "jump" through the air to the doorknob. Zap! You feel a shock.

**Solve This!**

**3** Suppose you comb your hair and electrons move from your hair to the comb. Will the comb now have a positive, negative, or neutral charge? How about your hair?

A discharge of static electricity can be seen as a spark—often a dramatic one.

# Electric Current

Protons and neutrons are locked in place in an atom's nucleus—they don't move around much. But electrons have a lot of energy and move rapidly around the nucleus. Electrons usually stay within the atom. But sometimes they get pulled away, and jump from one atom to another. In this way, electrons become a stream of electric charges that flow within a material.

Such a stream of flowing electric charges is called **electric current** or current electricity. Electric current is measured in units called **amperes** or amps.

Some materials allow electric current to pass through easily. Such materials are called **conductors**. Copper is a good conductor. Electrical wiring is often made of copper.

**Solve This!**

**4** Suppose a current of 2 amps is flowing through wire A, a current of 4 amps is flowing through wire B, and a current of 12 amps is flowing through wire C.

a. How many times greater is the current in C than the current in A? The current in C than the current in B?
b. What is the ratio of the current in B to the current in A? B to C?

Metals such as copper are good conductors. That is why electrical wiring is usually made of copper. The wire is coated with plastic, which is an insulator. What might be the reason for this?

Other materials are electrical **insulators**—they do not allow current to flow through them very well. Rubber and wood are good insulators.

Conductors provide a path for electric charges to flow along. The path made by a conductor for current to move through is called a **circuit**. A circuit is a complete loop; there are no gaps in the conducting path. Current will not flow through a circuit unless it is complete, or closed.

**5** Batteries are sources of electric current. They give electric charges a push through a circuit.

Compare the lifetimes of the different batteries shown below. Do they last longer if they are left on or if they are used from time to time? Do all the brands work this way?

**AVERAGE LIFETIMES OF HEAVY-DUTY C BATTERIES**

| Brand | Battery stays on | Battery used from time to time |
|-------|------------------|--------------------------------|
| A | 6.6 hours | 58.2 hours |
| B | 5.8 hours | 52.4 hours |
| C | 7.2 hours | 66.3 hours |
| D | 3.8 hours | 45.4 hours |
| E | 3.9 hours | 44.6 hours |

## What Makes Electrons Flow?

The flow of electric charges—current—is a lot like the flow of water through a pipe. Water flows from one end of a pipe to the other because of a difference in pressure at the ends. Water goes from an area of high pressure to an area of low pressure.

In a similar way, current flows from an area of high electric pressure to an area of low electric pressure. But a different name is used for electric pressure—it is called electric **potential**.

When there is a difference in potential so that one end of a conductor is at a higher potential than the other, current will flow through the conductor. This difference in electric potential that causes current to flow is called **voltage**.

Alessandro Volta, born in 1745 in Italy, invented the electrophorus in 1775. This device generates and stores static electricity. In 1800, Volta invented the first electric battery, which enabled scientists to study current electricity. The volt, the unit of electric potential, is named in Volta's honor.

Solve This!

**6** Do you understand the difference between current and voltage? Look at the diagrams. They show four different combinations of current and voltage. Each student represents current. Each backpack represents voltage. Using the words "low" and "high," describe each diagram.

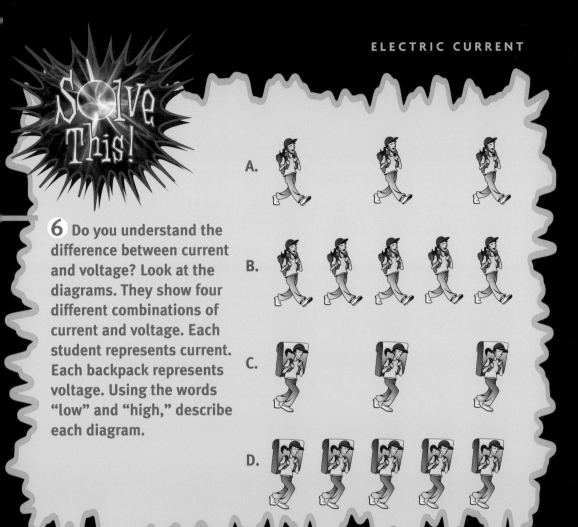

A.

B.

C.

D.

You can think of voltage as a "push" applied to electrons in a circuit. The higher the voltage, the stronger the push or pressure applied to each electron.

Don't confuse voltage with current. They are not the same thing. Voltage relates to the energy of each electron—how strongly it is pushed through the circuit. Current is a measure of the number of electrons moving and their speed. The diagrams above will help you understand how current differs from voltage.

## What Blocks Electron Flow?

What determines how much current will flow in a circuit? Naturally, part of the answer to this question is voltage. But there is something else. The other factor that determines current flow is called **resistance.** Resistance is the opposition of a material to the flow of electrons. The higher the resistance, the lower the current.

All materials, including good conductors, have some resistance. Resistance depends on the composition, length, thickness, and temperature of the conductor.

A typical circuit has many different parts, each with a different resistance. The current-carrying wires usually have low resistance. But a computer, lamp, or other appliance has high resistance. The unit of resistance is the **ohm**.

George Simon Ohm was born in Germany in 1787. He had a great talent for math but was not a serious student. He dropped out of college before getting a Ph.D. He taught high school physics and math. Luckily, he grew fascinated by electricity and later started the research that eventually led to Ohm's Law.

Radios, televisions, phones, and other electrical devices use circuit elements called resistors (right) to control the flow of current to different parts of their circuits.

## Voltage, Current, and Resistance Are Related

Perhaps you can now see that the current that flows through a circuit depends on the voltage and the resistance. A formula called **Ohm's Law** shows the relationship among voltage, resistance, and current. Ohm's Law states: current = voltage ÷ resistance. Two equivalent ways of expressing this formula are:

voltage = current x resistance and

resistance = voltage ÷ current.

Here's an example: Suppose a toaster has 20 ohms of resistance. How much current is passing through when a voltage of 120 volts is applied to the circuit? The formula to use is:

current = voltage ÷ resistance

current = 120 volts ÷ 20 ohms,

current = 6 amps.

So 6 amps of current is passing through the toaster.

How much current do these devices need to operate? It's easy to find the answer if you know voltage and resistance and use Ohm's Law.

**7** How much current passes through a lamp that has a resistance of 100 ohms when 50 volts is applied to the circuit?

# Two Kinds of Circuits

There are two kinds of circuits through which electricity can flow. They differ in how the devices that are part of the circuit are set up and how many paths along the circuit the current has to follow.

**Series Circuits**

Sometimes, there is only one path along which current can flow in a circuit. In this case, the electrons have to pass through everything in the loop. This type of circuit is called a **series circuit**.

Look at the diagram of a series circuit. The charges that flow from the battery have only one path to flow through. They must flow from the negative terminal of the battery through each light bulb and then to the positive terminal of the battery in order to make a closed circuit.

If one of the light bulbs in a series circuit burns out, no current can pass through it. A gap has been introduced in the conducting path. Current will not flow through any of the bulbs and they will not light up.

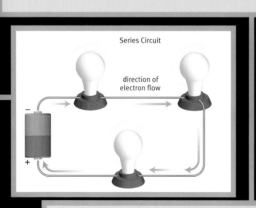

Series Circuit

direction of electron flow

In a series circuit, current has only one path to follow. Home and office security systems are wired in series. Can you explain why?

## S☀lve This!

**8** If three light bulbs are connected in series, what happens to the brightness of each bulb if another bulb is added to the circuit?

The total resistance that this circuit offers is the sum of the individual resistances of each element.

How much current flows through each bulb in a string of lights connected in series? Because current has only a single pathway, the current through each bulb must be the same. Current does not "get stuck" or "pile up" anywhere in the circuit.

How much resistance does a series circuit have? The current in a series circuit is resisted by the first device, the second device, and so forth.

So the total resistance is the sum of the individual resistances.

There is a "voltage drop" at each resistance. In other words, voltage is reduced at each resistance that current encounters on its way around the circuit. The total of all the voltage losses equals the initial voltage supplied to the circuit by the battery or other power source.

## Parallel Circuits

When you walk into the kitchen and turn on the light, do the toaster and stove turn on at the same time? They don't because they are not connected in series. These devices are wired in a different type of circuit—a **parallel circuit**.

The diagram shows three light bulbs wired in parallel.

In this arrangement, there is more than one possible path for current to take on its way around a closed loop. Can you see that the electric charges can pass through any one of the bulbs in the circuit and not the others yet still complete a closed path?

What would happen if one of the bulbs in a parallel circuit burned out? The other bulbs would stay lit. Each bulb operates on current in a different branch of the circuit. So each bulb operates independently.

In a parallel circuit, current can flow through more than one path on its way around the circuit.

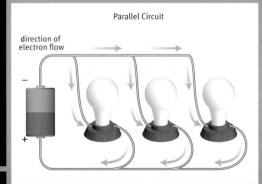

Parallel Circuit

direction of
electron flow

−

+

# Famous Firsts!

Thomas Alva Edison is a giant in the history of science and technology. Born in Ohio in 1847, he taught himself about electricity as a child. His first invention, a telegraph that printed stock prices, sold on Wall Street for a small fortune. With his profits, he started the first technology research laboratory in the United States. There, he invented the phonograph, the electric light, the first movies, and many other things, including wax paper. In all, he held about 1,100 patents.

Is the current in each branch of a parallel circuit the same? No, the total current divides into separate streams. Current flows most easily through devices with low resistance. This means the lower the resistance, the higher the current, and the higher the resistance, the lower the current. This follows Ohm's Law.

Here is an example. A lamp with 100 ohms of resistance is connected in parallel with a lamp with 50 ohms of resistance. How do the currents in the lamps compare? Ohm's Law says: current = voltage ÷ resistance. So the current through the 50-ohm lamp is double the current in the 100-ohm lamp.

**9** Two lamps are connected in parallel. One has 40 ohms of resistance; the other has 80 ohms of resistance. Which lamp will burn most brightly?

Solve This!

# From the Power Plant to Your Home

You've learned a lot about electricity so far: Streams of electric charges are electric current, and current moves through circuits that contain all sorts of appliances. Current carries electrical energy that the appliances use to operate. But where does the current that travels to these devices come from?

The electric current you use comes from either batteries or a wall plug. Batteries contain chemicals that take part in chemical reactions. The chemical reactions produce flowing electrons, or current. When you attach a battery to a flashlight, for example, charges flow from the battery through wires connected to the flashlight bulb. The current delivers energy to the light bulb and it lights up.

The source of electricity that operates a flashlight is a battery.

You also obtain electricity from wall outlets. Current travels to these outlets from a power plant.

Most power plants use heat to make electricity. To make the heat, coal, oil, or natural gas is burned. Some power plants get heat from nuclear reactions that take place in nuclear reactors.

Power plants that supply electricity to your home make huge amounts of power—and that is good. But they also pollute the air and consume valuable fossil fuels—and that is bad. Nuclear power plants make lots of electricity, too. But they create nuclear waste, which is a problem. There are cleaner ways to make electricity, as the photos show. Hopefully these alternative sources of electricity will become more widely available soon.

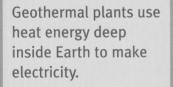

Solar generators collect energy from the Sun and transform it into electricity.

Geothermal plants use heat energy deep inside Earth to make electricity.

Windmills transform the energy of moving air, or wind, into electricity.

## Moving Electricity to Your Home

Power plants take energy from fossil fuels, nuclear reactions, or alternative sources like tides and convert it to electrical energy. That's the first part of the job. The second part is delivering the electrical energy to homes and factories where it can be used. How is this done?

Current travels through power lines that lead out of a power plant. The current leaves the plant at a very high voltage.

But it's still not high enough. The voltage must be increased to an even higher level so current can travel long distances without much waste of its precious cargo—electrical energy.

The problem is that current at such a high voltage is unsafe. So it must be changed, or transformed, to a lower voltage. A device, appropriately called a **transformer**, does the job. Transformers raise or lower voltage.

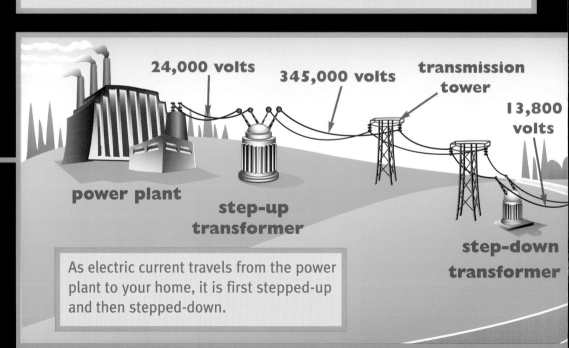

24,000 volts

345,000 volts

transmission tower

13,800 volts

power plant

step-up transformer

step-down transformer

As electric current travels from the power plant to your home, it is first stepped-up and then stepped-down.

A transformer consists of wires bent into coils and attached to a conductor. There is an input coil, called the primary. There is also an output coil, called the secondary. The voltage out of the secondary is "stepped up" (increased) or "stepped down" (decreased) compared to the primary.

There is a relationship between the number of wire loops in the primary and secondary and the voltage in and out of the transformer. It is:

$$\frac{\text{primary voltage}}{\text{number of primary loops}} = \frac{\text{secondary voltage}}{\text{number of secondary loops}}$$

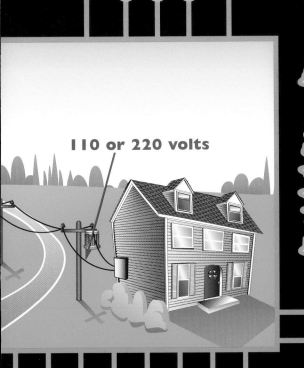

110 or 220 volts

**Solve This!**

**10** Suppose a transformer has a primary coil with 100 loops and a secondary with 200 loops. If a voltage of 100 volts is put across the primary, what will be the output voltage in the secondary? Is this a step-up or step-down transformer?

# Power and Energy

Current delivers electric energy, which is used in different ways. It can run an air conditioner, operate a video game, or move the blades of a fan. Do different devices all use equal amounts of electric energy? No, heating your home takes lots more energy than lighting a lamp, for example.

**Electric power** is the amount of energy that flows through a circuit in a given amount of time. In other words, it is a measure of how fast electrical energy is delivered. Electric power is measured in **watts**. To measure larger amounts of power, the **kilowatt** is used. A kilowatt is equal to 1,000 watts.

## Famous Firsts!

James Watt, famous as the almost-inventor of the steam engine, was born in Scotland in 1736. Watt was a sickly child. Unable to go to school regularly, he became his own teacher. He showed a talent for math and a great interest in the workings of machines. Accordingly, he started a business making mathematical instruments. In 1763, Watt was sent an early-model steam engine to repair. While doing this job, he quickly discovered how he could make the machine more efficient. Watt's version of the steam engine quickly became popular, replacing the earlier model. Later he improved his engine design again. Soon, Watt's patented engines were used for many kinds of industrial work.

Watt died a rich man at the age of 84. The unit of power, the watt, is named in his honor.

Electric energy and power are related by the following formula:

electric energy = electric power X time

Electric utility companies bill their customers according to how much energy is consumed. The unit used to measure electric energy is the **kilowatt-hour**. A kilowatt-hour is the energy consumed in one hour if the electric power is 1 kilowatt. Therefore, if a company charges 10 cents per kilowatt-hour, a 100-watt light bulb can run for 10 hours at a cost of 10 cents, or 1 cent per hour. A toaster or iron uses more electric energy and power than a light bulb, so it costs more to run it.

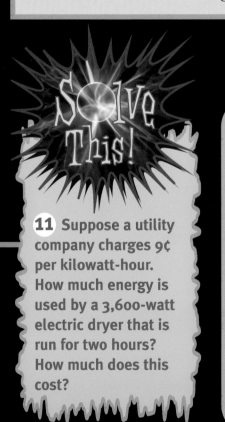

**11** Suppose a utility company charges 9¢ per kilowatt-hour. How much energy is used by a 3,600-watt electric dryer that is run for two hours? How much does this cost?

ELECTRIC USE - RATE EL1  RESIDENTIAL

```
09/23/03 reading (Actual).......  36643
08/22/03 reading (Actual)....... -36421

Total KWH used in  32 days......    222
```

CHARGES FOR ELECTRICITY USED

```
Basic service charge:              $10.89
  (does not include usage)
             KWH     COST/KWH
First       222.0 @ 10.0000¢       22.00
Adjust. Factor    @  1.5450¢        3.43
Sales tax @  2.5000%                 .91
```

CURRENT ELECTRIC CHARGES           $37.23

## Conserving Electricity

Electricity enables us to live longer, healthier, more enjoyable lives. But there is a cost. As you have learned, much of the electricity we use comes from burning fossil fuels. Fossil fuels are in short supply. Other sources of electricity produce pollution and toxic wastes. Still others are not available on a large scale.

Common sense tells us that it is essential to use electricity wisely. We must conserve it now so that future generations can enjoy the same benefits we do without serious damage to the environment. Here are some conservation tips:

• Turn off all lights when you leave a room.
• Turn off the TV, radio, and computer when you are finished with them.
• Ask your parents to replace regular light bulbs with special "compact fluorescent lights." They use only 25 percent of the energy of regular bulbs.

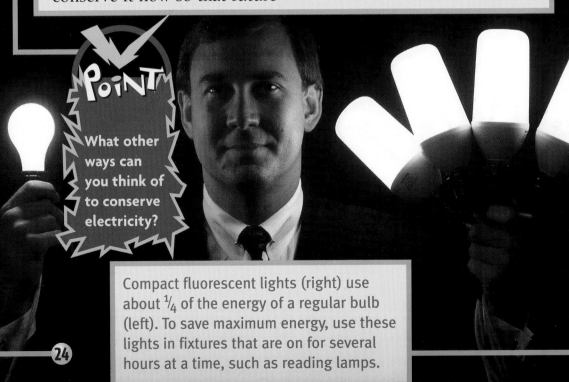

**Point**

What other ways can you think of to conserve electricity?

Compact fluorescent lights (right) use about ¼ of the energy of a regular bulb (left). To save maximum energy, use these lights in fixtures that are on for several hours at a time, such as reading lamps.

**12** Examine this bar graph. List the devices you use. What are the 5 biggest electricity consumers on your list?

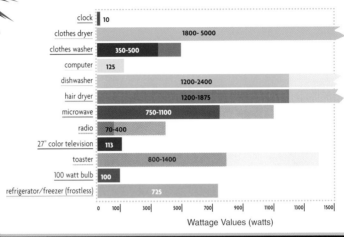

| Device | Wattage |
|---|---|
| clock | 10 |
| clothes dryer | 1800- 5000 |
| clothes washer | 350-500 |
| computer | 125 |
| dishwasher | 1200-2400 |
| hair dryer | 1200-1875 |
| microwave | 750-1100 |
| radio | 70-400 |
| 27" color television | 113 |
| toaster | 800-1400 |
| 100 watt bulb | 100 |
| refrigerator/freezer (frostless) | 725 |

Wattage Values (watts)

0   100   300   500   700   900   1100   1300   1500

Most of the electricity you use at home goes to operate appliances that consume a lot of electicity. It would be almost impossible to do without many of these appliances. But energy consumption can be reduced by purchasing appliances with the ENERGY STAR® label. ENERGY STAR® appliances have been identified by the U.S. Environmental Protection Agency and the Department of Energy as being the most energy-efficient products in their classes.

This label appears only on the most energy-efficient appliances.

To conserve electricity find out where the greatest energy losses are in your home.

# Electric Safety

You should always use electricity carefully because it can be quite dangerous. One of the major hazards of electricity is fire; the other is electric shock.

**Keeping Circuits Safe**

All electric wires have some resistance. This causes some electric energy to be lost when current is flowing through them. The "lost" electric energy is converted to heat, and the wires heat up. If too much current flows through the wires, too much heat is produced. The wires can become so hot that a fire starts.

If many appliances are plugged into the same circuit and used at the same time, too much current may flow and start a fire. To prevent this, all circuits should have **fuses** or **circuit breakers**. These are devices that open up a gap in the conducting path when too much current is flowing. The current stops, the appliances shut off, and fire is prevented.

Fuses and circuit breakers protect electric circuits.

## It's a Fact!

Circuits in homes usually have circuit breakers that open when current is greater than 15 or 20 amperes. Most lights and appliances draw only a few amperes. But heaters and hair dryers can draw 10 or more amperes. If you use too many such appliances at the same time, you could "blow a fuse."

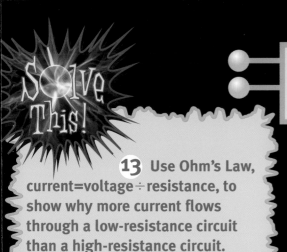
**13** Use Ohm's Law, current=voltage÷resistance, to show why more current flows through a low-resistance circuit than a high-resistance circuit.

Current flows along the unintended path formed by the crossing wires. This is a short circuit.

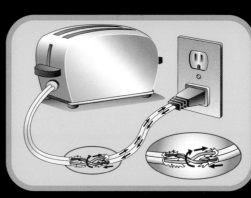

An electrical fire can also occur when there is a **short circuit**. A short circuit is an unintended pathway for current that has very low resistance. It can occur when two wires connected to an appliance touch before they reach the appliance.

Look at the diagram. The wires leading to and away from the toaster cross each other before reaching the toaster. Current takes the lowest-resistance path so it simply goes up to the point where the wires meet and back again to its source, avoiding the toaster completely. This short circuit would have very low resistance so a large current would flow through it. The circuit would quickly overheat and possibly catch fire.

Electric cords are usually covered with insulation to prevent the wires inside them from touching. If the insulation becomes damaged, a short circuit can occur. In this case a fuse or circuit breaker should shut off the current in the circuit. But if the fuses or breakers are faulty, there is a risk of fire. So cords with damaged insulation should be replaced.

## Avoiding Electric Shock

What causes electric shock? Electric shock is caused by current passing through your body. The current overheats body tissue and can upset the nerve center that controls your breathing and the normal rhythm of your heart.

Many people are killed every year because they handle common household appliances when they are touching or standing in water. Water is a good conductor. If you're wet, the electric resistance of your body is lowered. Current can flow from an appliance to your body to the water. This is the reason you should never use electric devices or touch sources of electricity such as outlets while you are in contact with water.

**14** A girl wants to play her electric guitar. She doesn't notice but the insulation on the electric cord of her guitar is frayed. When she plugs her guitar into the wall socket she receives an electric shock. The current in her body reaches 0.012 ampere. What is the effect on her body?

## Effects of Electric Shock on the Human Body

| Current (ampere) | Effect |
| --- | --- |
| 0.001 | Can be felt |
| 0.005 | Painful |
| 0.010 | Muscle spasms |
| 0.015 | Loss of muscle control |
| 0.070 | Probably fatal if current lasts for more than 1 second |

# It's a Fact!

The voltage difference between a cloud and the ground where lightning strikes is typically between 10 million and 100 million volts. An electric discharge this intense can heat the surrounding air to a white-hot 30,000°C!

A wire that's connected to a voltage source is called a live wire. Never touch a live wire. If you do, current will run through your body to the ground. You will become part of a circuit—a shocking experience! Depending on the voltage, it could be fatal.

Power lines carry current at a high voltage. Often these wires aren't insulated. Sometimes power lines fall to the ground in a storm. A fallen power line is an especially dangerous live wire. If you see a fallen power line, stay away from it. Contact the police or fire department.

Lightning is nature's most awesome display of electricity. But about 100 people in the United States are killed each year by lightning strikes. Many others are seriously injured. So remember the lightning safety rules:

• Don't stay outdoors. Go into a house or car.

• If you are outside, crouch but don't lie down. Your shoes are insulators so they can provide some protection from charges moving along the ground. Stay away from tall trees.

• Don't use appliances or the telephone.

• Don't go near water.

Electricity . . . use it, enjoy it, conserve it, and treat it with respect. It's a powerful force!

# Solve This! Answers

1. Page 3   Answers will vary.

2. Page 5 a.   79 electrons;
b. It will have a positive charge.

3. Page 7   The comb will have a negative charge; hair will have a positive charge.

4. Page 8   a. 6 times greater; 3 times greater;
b. 4 to 2, or 2 to 1; 4 to 12, or 1 to 3

5. Page 9   Batteries last longer if they are used from time to time. All the brands in the table behave in this way.

6. Page 11   a.  low current, low voltage;  b.  high current, low voltage;  c.  low current, high voltage;  high current, high voltage

7. Page 13   0.5 ampere

8. Page 15   The added light bulb makes all the bulbs in the circuit grow dimmer.

9. Page 17   The 40-ohm lamp will burn more brightly.

10. Page 21   200 volts; step-up transformer

11. Page 23
3,600 watts X 2 hours = 7,200 watt-hours = 7.2 kilowatt-hours. 7.2 kilowatt-hours X 9¢ per kilowatt-hour is approximately 65¢.

12. Page 25   Answers will vary.

13. Page 27   Ohm's Law shows that current and resistance are inversely proportional—the lower the resistance, the higher the current.

14. Page 28   According to the table, she experiences muscle spasms.

# Glossary

| | |
|---|---|
| ampere | (AM-peer) the unit of current (page 8) |
| circuit | (SER-kiht) a conducting pathway that current flows through (page 9) |
| circuit breaker | (SER-kiht BRAY-ker) a device that prevents excess current in a circuit by opening up a gap if excess current is present (page 26) |
| conductor | (kuhn-DUHK-ter) material that allows current to pass through it (page 8) |
| electric current | (ee-LEHK-trihk KUR-rent) stream of flowing electric charges (page 8) |
| electric power | (ee-LEHK-trihk POW-er) amount of energy delivered in a given time (page 22) |
| electron | (ee-LEHK-tron) tiny charged particle that flows to make electric current (page 4) |
| fuse | (FYOOZ) a device placed in a circuit to prevent excess current flow by melting if excess current is present (page 26) |
| insulator | (IN-su-lay-ter) material that tends to prevent current from passing through it (page 9) |
| kilowatt | (KIHL-oh-waht) 1,000 watts (page 22) |
| kilowatt-hour | (KIHL-oh-waht our) unit of electric power (page 23) |
| ohm | (OHM) the unit of electrical resistance (page 12) |
| Ohm's Law | (OHMZ LAW) voltage = current X resistance (page 13) |
| parallel circuit | (PAR-ah-lehl SER-kiht) a circuit that has more than one pathway for current to flow (page 16) |
| potential | (poh-TEN-shuhl) electric pressure (page 10) |
| resistance | (ree-ZIHS-tehns) the opposition of a material to the flow of charge (page 12) |
| series circuit | (SEER-eez SER-kiht) a circuit in which there is only one pathway for current to flow (page 14) |
| short circuit | (short SER-kiht) an unintended pathway for current that has very low resistance (page 27) |
| static electricity | (STAT-ihk ee-lehk-TRIHS-ih-tee) electric charge that builds up on an object and does not move (page 7) |
| transformer | (tranz-FOR-mer) a device that increases or decreases voltage (page 20) |
| volt | (VOHLT) unit of electric potential (page 10) |
| voltage | (VOHLT-ihj) a difference of electric potential that causes current to flow (page 10) |
| watt | (WAHT) the unit of power (page 22) |

# Index